Lerner SPORTS

SPORTS
ALL-ST★RS

JOSH ALLEN

Alexander Lowe

Lerner Publications ★ Minneapolis

SPORTS THRILLS *MEET* RESEARCH SKILLS

Lerner SPORTS

Free Database Trial: **lernersports.com**

Lerner Publications Company
An imprint of Lerner Publishing Group, Inc.
241 First Avenue North
Minneapolis, MN 55401 USA

For reading levels and more information, look up this title at www.lernerbooks.com.

Main body text set in Albany Std. Typeface provided by Agfa.

Library of Congress Cataloging-in-Publication Data

Names: Lowe, Alexander, author.
Title: Josh Allen / Alexander Lowe.
Description: Minneapolis : Lerner Publications, [2022] | Series: Sports all-stars (Lerner sports) | Includes bibliographical references and index. | Audience: Ages 7–11 | Audience: Grades 2–3 | Summary: "In 2020, quarterback Josh Allen led the Buffalo Bills to their first division title in 25 years. Allen grew up on a farm in California and starred at the University of Wyoming before joining the NFL"— Provided by publisher.
Identifiers: LCCN 2021035570 (print) | LCCN 2021035571 (ebook) | ISBN 9781728441191 (library binding) | ISBN 9781728449425 (paperback) | ISBN 9781728445151 (ebook)
Subjects: LCSH: Allen, Josh, 1996—-Juvenile literature. | Buffalo Bills (Football team)—Juvenile literature. | Quarterbacks (Football)—Biography—Juvenile literature. | Football players—United States—Biography—Juvenile literature.
Classification: LCC GV939.A534 L69 2022 (print) | LCC GV939.A534 (ebook) | DDC 796.33092 [B]—dc23

LC record available at https://lccn.loc.gov/2021035570
LC ebook record available at https://lccn.loc.gov/2021035571

Manufactured in the United States of America
1-49890-49733-7/15/2021

TABLE OF CONTENTS

Running to Victory 4

Facts at a Glance. 5

A Farm near Fresno. 8

Big Enough to Play 13

Taking Care of Business 18

What's Next? 24

All-Star Stats 28

Glossary 29

Source Notes 30

Learn More 31

Index 32

Josh Allen (*left*) avoids a tackle from an Indianapolis Colts defender.

The season was on the line for the Buffalo Bills. They faced the Indianapolis Colts in the National Football League (NFL) playoffs on January 9, 2021. With less than two minutes to go in the first half, the Colts were winning 10–7. The Bills were stuck far away from the end zone. Josh Allen, Buffalo's quarterback, knew he had to do something special to help the Bills take the lead.

- **Date of birth:** May 21, 1996

- **Position:** quarterback

- **League:** NFL

- **Professional highlights:** was the seventh overall pick in the 2018 NFL Draft; had 35 passing touchdowns and five rushing touchdowns in one season; led the Bills to the 2021 American Football Conference (AFC) championship game

- **Personal highlights:** grew up near Fresno, California; grew up on a farm; has a cereal named after him

Allen's arm strength has helped make him a successful passer in the NFL.

Allen took the snap. Colts defenders rushed at him. He threw the ball right before he was hit. It flew more than 30 yards. Gabriel Davis made the catch right on the edge of the field. The play gave the Bills a great chance to score.

The Bills had the ball at the five-yard line. But there were only 20 seconds left in the half. They would have to hurry to score.

Allen took the snap and ran. He went past one defender and then zoomed by another. Two more defenders tackled Allen, but it was too late. He was in the end zone for the touchdown! The Bills took the lead and went on to win 27–24. It was the first playoff victory for their young star quarterback, and the first time the Bills had won a playoff game since 1995.

Josh Allen is the only quarterback in NFL history with at least 4,500 passing yards, 35 passing touchdowns, and 5 rushing touchdowns in one season.

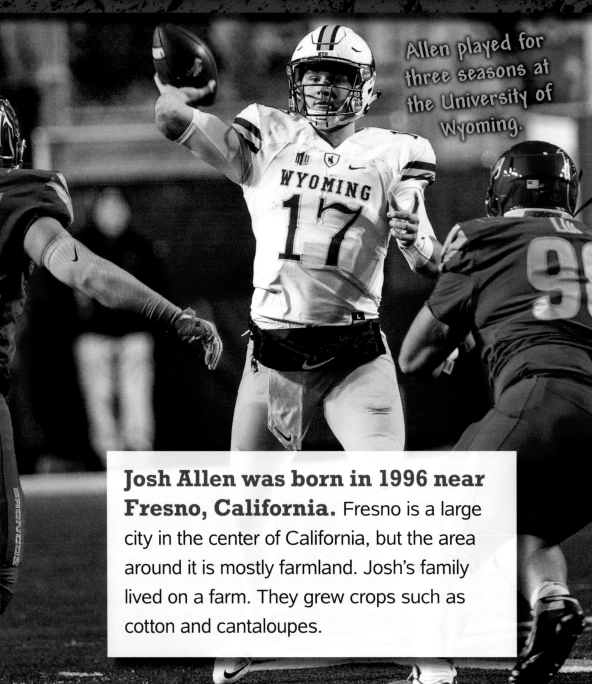

A FARM NEAR FRESNO

Allen played for three seasons at the University of Wyoming.

Josh Allen was born in 1996 near Fresno, California. Fresno is a large city in the center of California, but the area around it is mostly farmland. Josh's family lived on a farm. They grew crops such as cotton and cantaloupes.

Farmers in the Fresno area grow many different crops, especially almonds, grapes, and pistachios.

Josh grew up loving sports. He played basketball and baseball, but as he got older, he found that football was his true love. Unfortunately, he did not get any major scholarship offers to play college football. Josh was smaller than most college quarterbacks. He was 6 foot 3 (1.9 m), but he weighed 180 pounds (82 kg). Most college coaches didn't think he could handle playing against much bigger opponents.

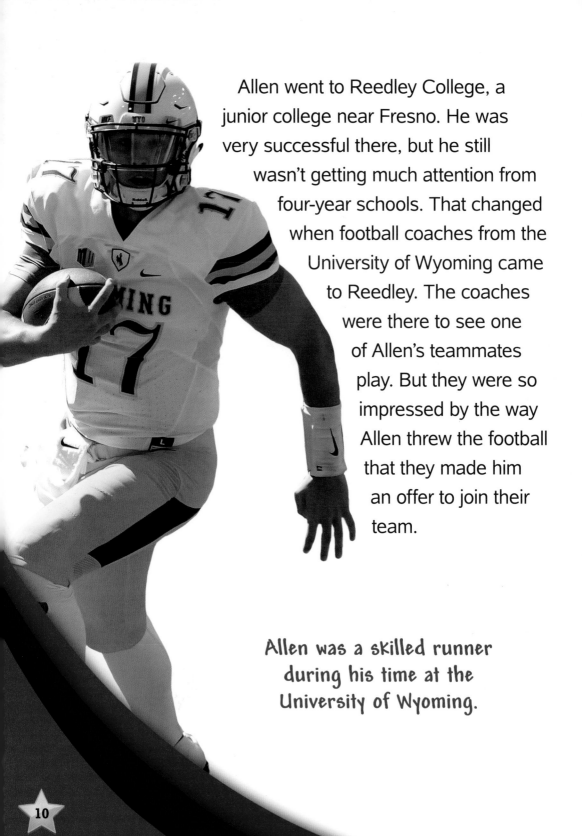

Allen went to Reedley College, a junior college near Fresno. He was very successful there, but he still wasn't getting much attention from four-year schools. That changed when football coaches from the University of Wyoming came to Reedley. The coaches were there to see one of Allen's teammates play. But they were so impressed by the way Allen threw the football that they made him an offer to join their team.

Allen was a skilled runner during his time at the University of Wyoming.

In his first season at Wyoming, Allen threw for over 3,000 yards and 28 touchdowns. He led his team to eight victories. "I was trying to show every college they made a mistake by not recruiting me," he said. "I played [mad] and I had a lot of success doing that."

Allen throws a pass for the University of Wyoming Cowboys.

Allen (left) was a first-round pick in the 2018 NFL Draft.

After his third season at Wyoming, Allen became a top NFL prospect. He decided to enter the 2018 draft. Fans weren't sure if Allen was ready to be a top pick, but many NFL teams were convinced. He was picked seventh overall by the Bills. Allen was ready for the NFL.

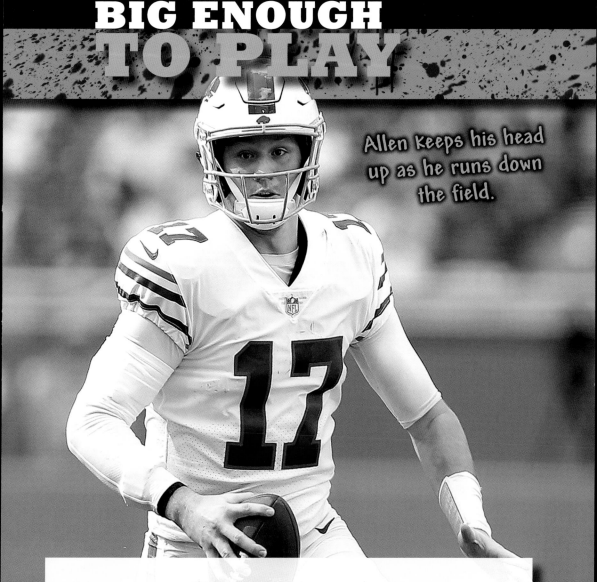

Allen keeps his head up as he runs down the field.

Allen always knew what it would take to play in the NFL. In college, he began lifting weights to get bigger and stronger. He bulked up to 237 pounds (107 kg), big enough to take on the toughest defenders.

Allen practices his passes during warm-ups before a game.

Allen spends each off-season working out and improving his quarterback skills. He works on his passing accuracy, his arm strength, and his leadership.

Allen works with quarterback coach Jordan Palmer. Allen started working with Palmer in 2018, before the draft. They have worked together every off-season since then.

Jordan Palmer was a member of the Bills in 2014, but he didn't play in any games.

"If you put a list together of the most physically talented players to ever play the position, I don't know who else is on that list, but (Allen) sure is," Palmer said. "He might be at the top of it."

Allen has worked on building bonds with his teammates.

Allen's biggest injury was a broken collarbone while he was in college. A defender hit him between Allen's helmet and shoulder pads. He had to have surgery to repair the bone. After surgery, Allen wore a sling and rested his arm for two weeks before he was able to move it and start lifting weights. He soon began throwing a football again.

In the 2020 off-season, the disease COVID-19 spread around the world and put sports on hold. Allen used this time to continue working on his passing. He also continued to be a leader for his team. He arranged workouts for his teammates to practice together. They worked on plays they planned to use during the next NFL season.

In 2019, Allen led the Bills to victory in five late-game comebacks.

Allen's popularity has risen as he has led the team to victories.

Allen celebrates a win with Bills fans.

Bills fans love their team's superstar players and support them on and off the field. As Buffalo's quarterback, Allen might be the most popular player on the team. That makes him attractive to companies who have something to sell.

Allen endorses Nike and wears the company's gear during games.

Allen is a big supporter of the John R. Oishei Children's Hospital.

Allen has a deal to endorse Nike products. That means the company pays him to wear Nike gear and appear in their ads. Allen also endorses New Era Cap. Since Allen is one of New Era's top NFL players, they asked him to design a special hat. Sales from Allen's hat helped benefit the John R. Oishei Children's Hospital (OCH).

In addition to endorsements, Allen looks for other ways to earn money. He owns part of OnCore Golf, a business that sells premium golf balls. Allen is a big fan of golf and plays often. He even gave some of his teammates custom golf balls and golf clubs as a gift for protecting him all season long.

In November 2020, Allen's grandmother died. He set up the Patricia Allen Fund at OCH in her honor. Many Bills fans donated money to the fund. They helped raise more than $1 million to pay for life-saving care for children. Officials named part of the hospital's tenth floor the Patricia Allen Pediatric Recovery Wing.

Josh's Jaqs is a special breakfast cereal named in Allen's honor. His picture is on the box, and some of the money from sales of the cereal goes to OCH.

Allen grows pistachio trees on his family's farm in California. He and his family are slowly turning 100 acres (40 ha) a year into pistachio farmland. They will soon have nearly 1,000 acres (405 ha) of pistachio trees.

Pistachio farmers have to be patient. The trees take five to seven years to produce seeds. Each acre (0.4 ha) of pistachio farmland can grow around 2,500 pounds (1,133 kg) of pistachios per year. Allen hopes that the farm can help make money for his family long after he is finished playing in the **NFL**.

Pistachios are nuts that grow on trees in groves.

Allen celebrates a playoff victory in 2021.

After beating the Colts in the 2021 playoffs, the Bills beat the Baltimore Ravens one week later. The next week, Buffalo fell to the Kansas City Chiefs. The Bills had not

Allen led the Bills to the 2021 AFC championship game against the Kansas City Chiefs.

advanced that far in the playoffs since the 1990s. But they fell short of their ultimate goal: winning the Super Bowl.

In 2021, the Bills extended Allen's contract for another six years. It was one of the biggest contract deals in NFL history. They believe he is the right quarterback to lead them to an NFL title.

Allen (*center*) hopes to use his speed and passing ability to keep the Bills at the top of the AFC.

Allen stands out from other players in the league. His speed makes him extremely hard to defend. Opponents are never sure whether Allen is going to throw the ball to a wide receiver or run for extra yards on his own. He has great leadership skills and one of the strongest throwing arms in the league. He can make short, quick passes or throw long balls deep down the field.

In the early 1990s, the Bills made it to the Super Bowl four years in a row. But they lost each time. Allen said he wants to lead the Bills to a Super Bowl title. "I don't ever want to leave, obviously," Allen said. "I want to play here for as long as I can and give back to the community."

The Bills are a team on the rise. Many fans think they have a great chance to finally win the Super Bowl. Allen's success has fans in Buffalo excited. With Allen leading the charge, the sky is the limit for the Bills.

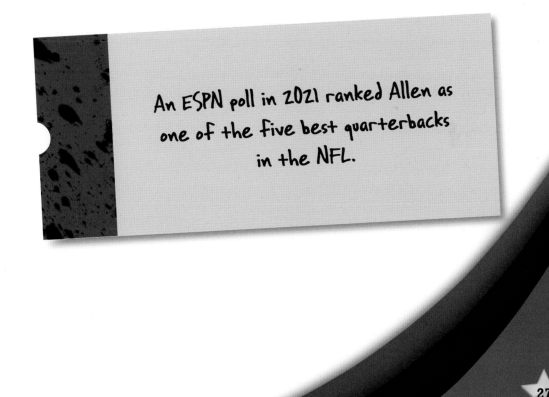

An ESPN poll in 2021 ranked Allen as one of the five best quarterbacks in the NFL.

All-Star Stats

One thing that sets Allen apart from many other quarterbacks is his ability to run with the ball. During the 2020 season, he set a new personal record for combined yards gained through the air and on the ground. Take a look at where Allen ranked in the NFL in 2020 in combined rushing and passing yards.

Top 10 Quarterbacks in Total Yards Gained in 2020

#	Player	Yards
1.	Deshaun Watson	5,267
2.	Patrick Mahomes	5,048
3.	Josh Allen	4,965
4.	Kyler Murray	4,790
5.	Russell Wilson	4,725
6.	Matt Ryan	4,673
7.	Tom Brady	4,639
8.	Justin Herbert	4,570
9.	Aaron Rodgers	4,448
10.	Kirk Cousins	4,421

Glossary

conference: one of two groups of teams (the AFC and the NFC) in the NFL

draft: when teams take turns choosing new players

end zone: the area at each end of a football field where players score touchdowns

endorse: to recommend something, such as a product or service, usually in exchange for money

junior college: a school that has two years of studies similar to those in the first two years of a four-year college

off-season: when a sports league is inactive

pistachio tree: a small Asian tree that produces edible greenish seeds

prospect: a player who is likely to succeed at a higher level of play

recruit: to find new players and get them to join a team or other group

scholarship: money that a school or another group gives to students to help pay for their education

snap: the act of putting the football in play by quickly passing it between the legs back to a teammate

Source Notes

11 Jeff Eisenberg, "How Wyoming's Josh Allen Went From Zero Scholarships to the Top of NFL Draft Boards," *Yahoo Sports*, August 17, 2017, https://www.yahoo .com/entertainment/wyomings-josh-allen-went-zero -scholarships-top-nfl-draft-boards-193456311.html

15 Wojton, Nick. "Jordan Palmer on Josh Allen: Might Be 'Most Physically Talented' QB Ever," *BillsWire*, February 18, 2021, https://billswire.usatoday.com/2021/02/18 /jordan-palmer-josh-allen-most-physically-talented-qb -rich-eisen-show/

27 Jourdon LaBarber, "I Don't Ever Want to Leave," *BuffaloBills.com*, November 11, 2020, https://www .buffalobills.com/news/josh-allen-reacts-to-outpouring-of -support-from-bills-mafia

American Football Facts for Kids
https://kids.kiddle.co/American_football

Buffalo Bills
https://www.buffalobills.com/

Josh Allen
https://www.buffalobills.com/team/players-roster/josh-allen/

Monson, James. *Behind the Scenes Football*. Minneapolis: Lerner Publications, 2020.

Scheff, Matt. *The Super Bowl: Football's Game of the Year*. Minneapolis: Lerner Publications, 2021.

Shulman, Mark. *The Story of the Buffalo Bills*. Minneapolis: Kaleidoscope, 2020.

Index

Buffalo Bills, 4–7, 12, 17, 19, 22, 24–25, 27

COVID-19, 17

Fresno, California, 5, 8, 10

John R. Oishei Children's Hospital, 21–22

National Football League (NFL), 4–5, 7, 12–13, 17, 21, 23, 25, 27

New Era Cap, 21

NFL Draft, 5, 12, 15

Nike, 21

OnCore Golf, 21

Palmer, Jordan, 15

Patricia Allen Fund, 22

Reedley College, 10

Super Bowl, 25, 27

University of Wyoming, 10–12

Photo Acknowledgments

Timothy T Ludwig/Stringer/Getty Images, p.4; Timothy T Ludwig/Stringer/Getty Images, p.6; Loren Orr/Stringer/Getty Images, p.8; Sam Wells/Getty Images, p.9; Steven Branscombe/Stringer/Getty Images, p.10; Sean M. Haffey/Staff/Getty Images, p.11; Tom Pennington/Staff/Getty Images, p.12; Michael Reave/Stringer/Getty Images, p.13; Michael Reaves/Stringer/Getty Images, p.14; Vaughn Ridley/Stringer/Getty Images, p.15; Tom Szczerbowski/Stringer/Getty Images, p.16; Timothy T Ludwig/Stringer/Getty Images, p.18; Tom Szczerbowski/Stringer/Getty Images, p.19; Jamie Squire/Staff/Getty Images, p.20; Andrew nyr/Wikimedia, p.21; GomezDavid/Getty Images, p.23; Bryan M. Bennett/Stringer/Getty Images, p.24; Jamie Squire/Staff/Getty Images, p.25; Elsa/Staff/Getty Images, p.26

Cover: Ralph Freso/Stringer/Getty Images